A CAREER AS A PIPELAYER

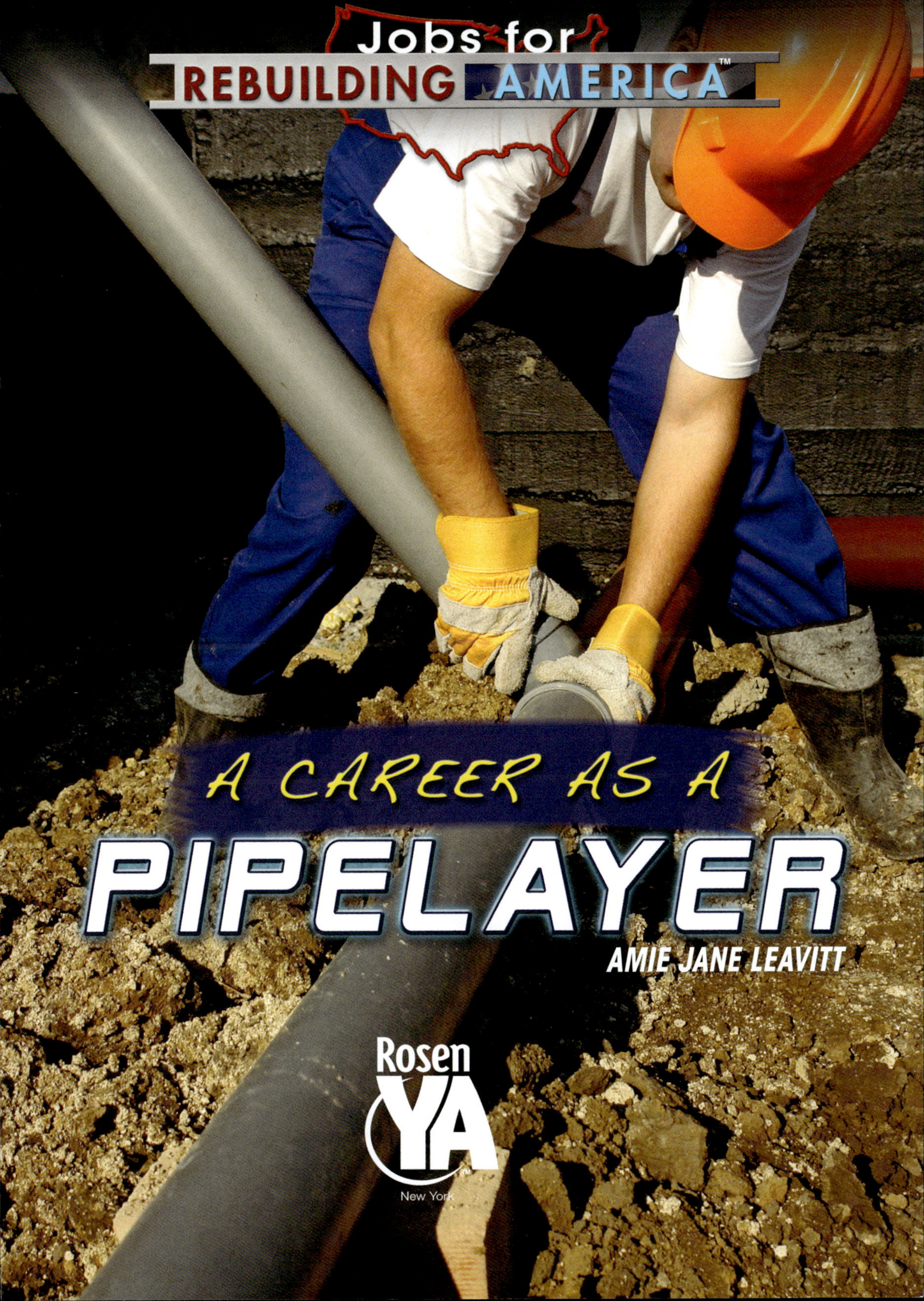

Jobs for REBUILDING AMERICA™

A CAREER AS A PIPELAYER

AMIE JANE LEAVITT

Rosen YA™

New York

Published in 2019 by The Rosen Publishing Group, Inc.
29 East 21st Street, New York, NY 10010

First Edition

Library of Congress Cataloging-in-Publication Data

Names: Leavitt, Amie Jane, author.
Title: A career as a pipelayer / Amie Jane Leavitt.
Description: New York : Rosen Publishing, 2019. | Series: Jobs for rebuilding America | Includes bibliographical references and index. | Audience: Grades 7–12.
Identifiers: LCCN 2017052858| ISBN 9781508179887 (library bound) | ISBN 9781508179894 (pbk.)
Subjects: LCSH: Underground pipelines—Design and construction—Vocational guidance—Juvenile literature.
Classification: LCC TA660.P55 L43 2019 | DDC 621.8/672—dc23
LC record available at https://lccn.loc.gov/2017052858

Manufactured in the United States of America

CONTENTS

INTRODUCTION

It is 6:15 a.m., and Ryley grabs breakfast at a drive-through on his way to the job site. For the past two years, Ryley has been working as a pipelayer, and each job that he's had so far has had slightly different start and end times. For this particular project, work begins promptly at 7 a.m. every morning, five days a week. The foreman is a stickler on tardiness, so Ryley always makes sure he is on the road with plenty of time to account for any kind of traffic issues that may arise along the way.

Ryley pulls into the job site a little early at 6:45 a.m. He parks his truck, clocks-in at the

Two city workers team up to repair a water main. Without the expertise of such workers to handle pipes both within and outside of homes, modern life would certainly be very different.

supervisor's work trailer, and then grabs his construction vest, hard hat, and gloves to join the rest of the pipelaying team who have assembled near the heavy equipment. Before work ended yesterday, the heavy equipment operator dug the trench they would be working in today. Unfortunately, it rained a little last night, so now the trench is a bit marshy. But those kinds of conditions don't phase Ryley in the least. He enjoys each part of his responsibilities, even stomping through the mud when he has to.

Today, the team is installing a storm drain pipe. Ryley and two other coworkers hop down into the tunnel. Other coworkers on the topside of the trench hook chains to a massive cement pipe that is 48 inches (1.2 meters) in diameter. Then, they hook the other end of the chains to the bucket of the excavator.

The excavator operator slowly lifts the pipe into the air and lowers it into the trench. The coworkers on the topside of the trench help spin the pipe around so the correct side is facing the pipe that has already been installed. As it's lowered, Ryley and the topside coworkers guide it into place, giving directions to the excavator operator to move it to the right, to the left, up, or down. The goal is to get the end of this new section to fit securely into the end of the previously installed pipe. Once the section is in place and snug like a glove, the chains are removed. Then, the process starts all over again until the entire storm drain pipe network is installed in this particular trench. More trenches are then dug by the excavator until the pipe network is complete. For this particular job, completion of the entire trench network will be weeks down the road.

In the late afternoon, Ryley is scheduled to receive training on the heavy equipment. Some of the operators are retiring by the end of the year and Ryley hopes to have expanded his skill set so he can take on one of those positions once they open up. Heavy equipment operation takes a great amount of skill, dexterity, and practice in order to become proficient. And only proficient operators are allowed to have control of such expensive and potentially dangerous machines, especially when they're lowering huge pipes over the top of coworkers in trenches. Ryley practices on one of the smaller machines, working on mastering the controls, lifting objects, and digging small holes and trenches. The foreman said he can move on to practicing on some of the larger equipment tomorrow.

By 4:00 p.m., Ryley and his coworkers have put in a full day's work. Some days, they have to work extra hours and thereby qualify for overtime, especially when the project deadline is looming. But not today. They're lucky enough to hit the road before the evening rush-hour traffic gets too bad.

CHAPTER ONE

BUILDING AMERICA: THE WORLD UNDER OUR FEET

As a pipelayer, Ryley works in the world of infrastructure. Infrastructure includes many different types of jobs, which are essentially those that build the foundations of cities, states, regions, or nations. Specifically as a pipelayer, Ryley works in the public works segment of infrastructure, which includes storm drain, sewer, water, and also piped-fuel systems.

A BRIEF HISTORY OF PIPING

The history of using pipes to transport water, waste, and other materials can be traced all the way back to the ancient world. The ancient Egyptians used clay and copper pipes to transport water and waste. The Chinese used large sections of hollow bamboo as pipes for the same purpose. However, it's believed that they also used their pipes to transport natural gas, too. The ancient Mesopotamians used underground tunnels called qanats—which are essentially large, earthen pipes—to move water from aquifers to farms, homes, and cities. The ancient Indus Valley civilizations—modern-day India—also used piping systems to transport water and waste to and from large cities. The Romans were famous for the aqueducts, which stretched across their massive empire. Some aqueducts were 60 miles (97 kilometers) long. They were used to transport water from springs in the mountains to urban areas in drier geographical areas.

Just because pipes were used in ancient times certainly doesn't mean they were the norm. Very few people had access

Ancient Rome is famous for many things, including its impressive engineering feats. This illustration shows a segment of its aqueduct network, which extended all throughout the Roman Empire.

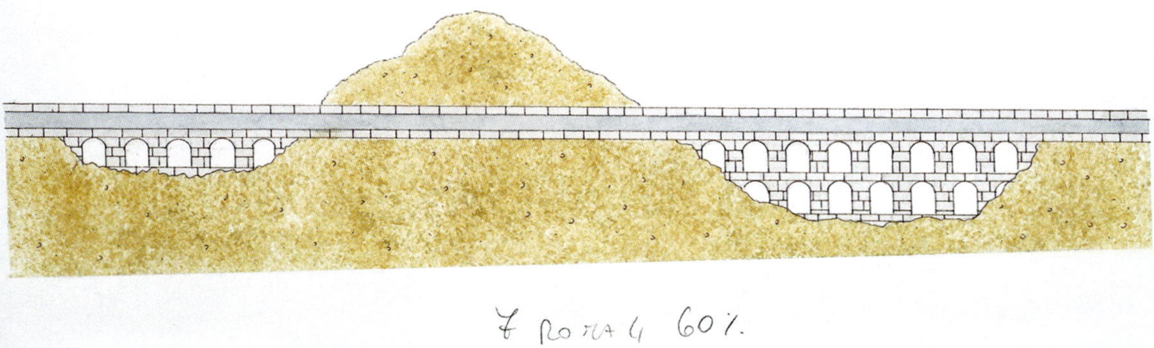

to these types of systems. Most of the world's population had to carry their water from nearby rivers, lakes, and streams to use for washing, drinking, and cooking. And, as far as disposing of waste, they used outdoor restroom facilities or tossed out waste that was collected indoors.

In urban areas, wastewater (from storms and restroom facilities) often flowed in open ditches through the city streets to nearby water supplies. Keep in mind that quite often this was the same water supply used for the population's washing, drinking, and cooking.

These particular methods of retrieving water and disposing of waste are highly unsanitary and often led to major health problems, including outbreaks of diseases such as typhoid and cholera. Therefore, when piping systems were incorporated into a community to bring fresh water and dispose of waste, the overall health and standard of living of the population dramatically improved.

PIPES AND MATERIALS

In the past, pipes have been made from stone, clay, bamboo, metal, and even hollowed-out logs. Modern pipes are made out of many different types of materials, including prefabricated concrete, stone, metal (steel, copper, cast iron), and plastic, namely polyvinyl chloride, or PVC.

The type of pipe used by pipe workers varies depending upon where the pipe will be used and what it will carry. For example, a pipe in the ground that needs to transport large

Sections of polyvinyl chloride pipe, commonly known as PVC pipe, are shown here. Workers in this industry have to handle piping of various sizes, which are often fitted at different angles.

quantities of storm water needs to be strong, large in diameter, and long lasting. Therefore, a narrow, thin-walled PVC pipe wouldn't be used for this type of system. Instead, a massive prefabricated cement pipe would be a better choice for this type of project. In contrast, water moved from one room to another inside a house wouldn't need to move about in a massive cement pipe. In this situation, a smaller PVC pipe would be best to install.

TOOL FEATURE: LASER LEVELS

Installing pipe isn't as simple as digging a trench, inserting the pipe, and then covering it with soil. One of the main considerations to account for is the principle of slope. Materials can only be moved through a pipe in one of two ways: by the effects of gravity or by force applied through a pump. Most pipes in the ground allow materials to flow by using the principle of gravity.

In order to utilize the effects of gravity, the pipe must have a slight downhill slope to it. In other words, if you want to move a material from point A to point B in a pipe, point A must be slightly higher in elevation than point B. Or, point A must slope downward toward point B. This allows the earth's gravity to pull on the materials and cause them to move through the pipe. Not only does the beginning need to be higher than the ending of the pipe, the fall must also stay consistent throughout the length of the pipe. If the pipe dips upward at all or remains on a flat horizontal plane, then material flowing through the pipe could clog in those sections and cause backups. And a backup is definitely not something you want to have happen when transporting sewage or other wastewater.

Slope in a pipe is determined using a variety of tools, including a laser level. This device has two main parts: a transmitter on a tripod and a receiver on a measuring stick. The two are set up at varying distances from each other. The transmitter sends a beam of red light toward the receiver. The receiver beeps when the beam of light strikes it. Then, the workers make calculations and use mathematics to determine the slope of the pipe. Adjustments are then made to the trench to either raise or lower the pipe in order to achieve the proper slope. The laser level is an ideal tool to determine slope due to light's two main properties: it travels in a straight line and it can travel infinite distances.

In addition to their use in pipelaying, laser levels are used in site grading, concrete work, fence construction, foundations, and so forth. Therefore, when a trades worker learns how to use a laser level, that person is making himself or herself more marketable across the construction industry.

Remember that pipes aren't just long tubes that carry water and waste. They also carry gases, fuel, acids, chemicals, and any other type of liquid that needs to be transported from one place to another. Pipes that carry these types of materials need to be specially designed and made out of particular materials so the

Larger, more complex types of piping are crucial for commercial and industrial sites. These pipes are often made of steel or other durable materials and are used to transport a variety of different fluids (liquids and gases).

chemicals cannot erode them over time and cause hazardous conditions due to eventual leaks in the pipes.

WORKING WITH PIPES

Due to the various types of pipes and the many different materials they carry, people who work in this industry must have specific training and skills. There are three different types of workers that install pipes in infrastructure: pipelayers, pipefitters, and plumbers. One component that all three trade jobs have in common is that they involve both pipes and valves. The major difference between the jobs is that they each have specific responsibilities associated with those pipes and valves.

Pipelayers are the workers who install the pipes in or on the earth, and as a result generally work outdoors. In contrast, pipefitters and plumbers install and repair the pipes inside buildings, planes, and ships.

The main difference between pipefitters and plumbers is the types of systems and materials that they work with. Pipefitters generally work with more complex systems and hazardous materials. They work with high pressure and steam systems, hydraulics, and refrigeration. As a result, they generally work on commercial projects. Plumbers usually work on pipes that carry water and waste. They work on both commercial and residential projects.

A JOB THAT MAKES A DIFFERENCE

Most people don't often consider how important jobs are in this industry. When something is out of sight and out of mind, like our nation's infrastructure, it's easy to take it for granted. So, just take a moment and think about it right now. Think about how pipelaying jobs, in particular, benefit you in your daily life.

The job is directly responsible for most people having access to fresh water. What would your life be like today if

Workers often use heavy construction equipment and vehicles to maneuver large pipe sections and other pieces of infrastructure into place. It is a job that requires skill, care, and patience.

there were no underground pipe networks to bring fresh, clean water to your house? How would you get your water to drink, cook, wash, or bathe? Would you have to walk miles to the nearest watering hole and carry buckets of water back to your home? How would this affect the many other things you'd prefer doing with your time? What if the water wasn't clean in the water source but it was the only water available to you? How would this affect your overall health?

Sanitation and waste disposal are other things that depend on the work of pipelayers. What would life be like if you no longer had a sewer system connected to your home? You could no longer just flush bathroom or other waste down a drain and have a pipe haul it away for you. What would you do instead? Would you have to dig a hole in the yard and have an old-fashioned outhouse instead? What if you lived in a city? Where would the facilities be located for your use? How would losing the access to an indoor bathroom affect your quality of life?

Imagine, also, that every time it rained, the storm water rose up and flooded your house instead of flowing down an underground network of storm drains. It would be a constant and nagging worry that you would have to anticipate possible flooding every time the clouds grew dark.

Finally, consider what your life would be like if you didn't have easy access to fuel for your automobiles or to heat your home. How would your daily routines be affected? Maybe you personally don't need fuel for those reasons, but what about the trucks that bring the food you eat to the grocery stores and restaurants? If those vehicles do not have easy access to fuel, you will not have as many options of things to buy or ease of purchasing them.

Underground utility work takes a lot of coordination in big urban areas like New York City. Roads, or at least parts of them, need to be temporarily blocked off so that workers can repair or install pipes below the asphalt.

CHANGING THE WORLD

Taking the time to think about life in these terms definitely helps you realize how crucial jobs in infrastructure are for our modern existence. Essentially, having the easiest possible access to what are considered the basic necessities of life (clean water and sanitation services) is what separates the developed world from other places. Countries that do not have adequate infrastructure in place are hard pressed to offer the same quality of life to most or all of their citizens.

Such factors can really harm the living standards and opportunities of the people who live with bad or nonexistent infrastructure. Individuals in undeveloped regions may have less time for school, work, and leisure because so much of their time is spent dealing with obtaining their basic needs. Their overall health is also negatively impacted because without access to fresh water, sanitation services, and storm drains, diseases are more common.

When one thinks about infrastructure in this way, it's easy to see how jobs in this industry can be extremely rewarding. People employed in these types of jobs are contributing in a measurable way to the health, well-being, and overall wealth of the country they live in. We as a society most definitely need people who are willing to dedicate their careers to jobs in infrastructure.

CHAPTER TWO

HAVING WHAT IT TAKES

Every type of job requires a certain aptitude, skill set, and level of enthusiasm. When people try to decide what type of career to pursue in life, it's important for them to know some basics about the job so they can assess whether or not it will be a good fit for them. To do this, individuals should look at various factors of jobs, including working conditions, responsibilities, required skills and training, and the necessary physical abilities and personality traits.

THE GREAT OUTDOORS

It's fair to assume that most or all of a pipelayer's work day will be spent outside in the elements. The only exception would be for time spent in a work trailer at meetings. During a typical workday, pipelayers will either be working inside the trenches installing the pipe, working with tools to determine grade and slope, or sitting inside the cabs of the heavy equipment digging the trenches, lifting, and setting the pipe.

The people who thrive in this type of job love spending time outdoors and completing new hands-on tasks every day.

Teamwork is essential when working on piping and other infrastructure jobs. Getting along with fellow workers is crucial to making that teamwork possible.

Since pipe is often installed year-round in most climates, pipelayers work in all types of weather conditions. In places that have four seasons, it might be blazing hot for part of the year, rainy and muddy for another part, and snowy and slushy for another. Individuals who prefer working indoors, or even in an office, where temperatures are constant and weather is not a factor, will likely be unhappy with life as a pipelayer.

A MULTIFACETED JOB

By just reading the word "pipelaying," one might assume that this job only has one main role—laying pipe. However, that isn't the case. Pipelaying does consist of laying pipe; however, there is much more to it than just this simple-sounding one-step task. Pipelayers also must know how to dig trenches, both by hand and also with the use of heavy equipment. Other important parts of the job are reading blueprints to ensure the trenches are dug in the proper location and finding existing

Pipeline work might include welding pipes inside a natural gas reservoir, as this photo shows. These employees are working on the Kara Sea shoreline, on the Yamal Peninsula, located in the Siberian region of Russia.

pipes using specialized equipment. They must also properly install the pipes in the ground, connect new pipes to existing ones, make sure the pipes have proper slope, and be able to adjust trenches to accommodate for slope requirements.

In addition to laying pipes on dry land, other pipelayers also work at installing fuel pipelines in ocean water. People who work in these types of jobs must have similar abilities, except they will not be doing any trench work, obviously. They also must know how to operate the equipment aboard the ship and use computer technology to lay the pipe in the correct location.

A LITTLE KNOW-HOW: MACHINERY AND TOOLS

While not all pipelayers will work on heavy equipment, those doing this job need to have an appreciation for these types of machines and a desire to eventually learn how to operate them. Working with heavy equipment is an important part of pipelaying. These big rigs grade the earth, dig the trenches, lift and lower the pipes, and fill the trenches once the pipes are completely installed and at the proper slope.

Heavy equipment operators generally make a higher wage than the base-level pipelayer working on the ground, too. Knowledge of specialized equipment often raises a pipelayer's pay grade up a notch or two. Pipelayers are also required to use additional tools, like laser levels, transit levels, magnetic or radio indicators (to find existing pipes), grade rods, tamping machines, and so forth.

OUT AT SEA

There are plenty of opportunities to lay pipe out at sea. These pipes bring liquid fuel and gases from offshore drills to shore. Generally, ships that lay pipe operate in groups of three. The first ship conducts an analysis of the sea floor. One way of performing this task is to lower a robotic submarine drone to the ocean floor, which moves about, gathering data. The information attained helps the pipeline company determine what type of pipe to use and how to install it.

The next two ships run in pairs. One ship is a barge—a flat-topped watercraft—that carries the long pipes. The other ship is the actual pipelaying vessel. It is equipped with the specialized machinery (such as cranes, robotic arms, and booms) that lifts the pipes off of the barge, moves them about on the ship, and then eventually lowers them into the sea.

A variety of workers are employed on these vessels. Maintenance crews ensure the machinery stays operational. Computer engineering crews operate the machines using specialized software. Navigation crews guide the ship to its desired location. Catering crews provide the food for the workers on the ships.

Construction crews on board have many responsibilities. Some might help attach massive chains to the pipes so the machines can transport the pipes from barge to ship. On some ships, robotic arms might do most of that task while construction crews stand by to oversee the job. Crews also work inside the ship on the ends of the pipes. They bevel, buff, heat, and weld the pipe ends, or make sure the machines are performing these tasks correctly. They also inspect the pipes to make sure they are up to code. Oceangoing pipelaying crews generally work twelve-hour shifts and can be out to sea for several weeks at a time.

STRENGTH AND AGILITY

The physical requirements for pipelaying can often be demanding. Pipelayers must be able to lift certain pipes of varying length and size. Granted, they won't be required to lift the large cement storm drain pipes—heavy equipment is used for that. But they will have to lift smaller pipes and readjust them inside trenches.

In addition, pipelayers also need to be able to shovel sand and gravel under a pipe to raise the slope or dig a trench by hand to lower the slope for a pipe. Shoveling might not sound so physically demanding, but even a half hour of it can really tax one's shoulder, back, arm, and leg muscles.

Pipelaying requires physical strength. People interested in this line of work should consider working out in advance of finding a job to get their bodies into the physical condition required for the tasks they'll be asked to do.

Along with physical strength, agility is another requirement for the job. Pipelayers often have to climb in and out of trenches frequently throughout a workday. When heavy pipes are being lifted overhead, workers also need to be quick on their feet to help guide the pipes into place and move out of the way so the heavy equipment operators can efficiently do their job.

QUIZ: IS THIS TYPE OF JOB FOR ME?

Take this quiz to determine your aptitude for a job as a pipelayer.

1. Do you like working outside?	YES	NO
2. Do you like working in different types of weather conditions?	YES	NO
3. Do you like learning new skills every day on the job?	YES	NO
4. Do you like working as part of a team?	YES	NO
5. Can you easily communicate with others?	YES	NO
6. Can you make decisions in difficult situations easily?	YES	NO
7. Do you enjoy working with machines?	YES	NO
8. Do you like measuring things and doing math problems?	YES	NO
9. Do you like to do things that help others?	YES	NO
10. Are you able to lift heavy things?	YES	NO
11. Are you able to climb in and out of trenches?	YES	NO
12. Are you a good problem solver?	YES	NO

If you answered "yes" to at least eight of the twelve questions, you will likely enjoy a job in the pipelaying industry. Remember, if you answered "no" to questions 5, 6, 8, 10, 11, and 12—these are all things that you can improve upon through classes, workshops, and personal enrichment.

COMMUNICATION SKILLS

Pipelaying requires teamwork. Everyone works more safely and efficiently when each person on the job can easily communicate ideas, instructions, and concerns to others. Most of it is good verbal communication. However, you also need to be able to use phone, email, and text to do your job. Talking and writing well are key, but so are good listening and reading comprehension skills. People in this job need to pay attention to and comprehend what they're being told. They should also be able to read and understand different kinds of materials, including blueprints and job orders.

Here are a few examples of how pipelayers may use communication in their jobs:

1. A pipelayer by a trench needs to tell the heavy equipment operator which direction to move the bucket so the pipe will match up with another pipe that is already in the trench.
2. A supervisor needs to train a new pipelayer on how to use the laser level to measure and calculate slope.
3. A pipelayer has to talk to his or her foreman about some safety concerns on the job site.
4. An employee must email the human resource department about a problem with a paycheck.
5. A worker needs to text a coworker to see if he or she can take a shift if an emergency arises.
6. A pipelayer is attending a work meeting and needs to pay attention to the instructions for the job site for that day.

Algebra, geometry, and other high school math might seem unnecessary, but these skills are essential for infrastructure-related careers. You'll likely use math (and logic and reasoning) every day on the job as a pipelayer.

7. An employee receives an email from the corporate office and needs to respond to some of the questions about a health insurance matter.
8. A trench worker needs to record measurements and slope calculations for use by the heavy equipment operator.

NUMBER SENSE

Math teachers, since probably the beginning of time, have heard this common complaint from their students: "Why do I have to learn this? I'm never going to use this!" While there may be some jobs out there where people do not have to use mathematics, pipelaying is definitely not one of them. Math is used constantly in pipelaying. Workers in this field need to be able to use measurement skills when cutting pipe. They must know how to take proper measurements using laser and traditional levels. In addition, they have to know how to properly add various measurements over long distances to figure out how long and deep to dig trenches. Workers must also know how to take the measurements and make calculations with them. They should be prepared to use formulas to configure proper slope for a long length of pipe and also how to figure how to adjust trenches when slope is too great, too shallow, and too level.

QUICK DECISION-MAKING

Pipelayers must know how to make decisions quickly on the spot and be adept at problem-solving. This is especially true when dealing with heavy equipment and expensive pipe segments.

For example, a pipelayer needs to be able to quickly figure out how to adjust a pipe so it slides adjacent to an already installed trench. A pipelayer also needs to figure out how to adjust the slope of a pipe by either adding or removing soil from a trench. Time is money on a construction site, so the

Writing skills are also essential in construction. You may have to compose emails to employers, draft instructions for coworkers, and explain complicated blueprints to employees and other workers.

faster a pipelayer can make these types of decisions, the happier the foreman and company will be.

This ability to make decisions quickly is also important when dealing with safety on the job. A pipelayer needs to be able to recognize possible dangerous situations and get himself or herself (and coworkers) out of the way to prevent accidents. This is especially true of any job that involves heavy equipment, heavy parts being lifted into the air, and any kind of trench work.

CHAPTER THREE

PIPELAYING 101

For many entering the construction sector, their first job will probably be as a laborer. Laborers are entry-level positions that often require a lot of hands-on, basic tasks. In pipelaying jobs, people who have no experience are quite often handed a shovel and shown where they can assist in trench digging and leveling.

Of course, people could theoretically stay in this role forever if they want. There's no shame in that. For many workers, however, there comes a time when they want a little something different to do to mix up their workday. In pipelaying, there are many other tasks to perform and a worker will get on-the-job training for those. Most workers never do the same task all the time, day in and day out. Additional tasks include operating the laser level and knowing how to use a transit level, compacting the soil with tamping machines, and using magnetic or radio indicators to find existing pipes in the ground.

GETTING THE BASICS IN HIGH SCHOOL

High school students who are interested in becoming pipelayers after graduation should take some time while in school to attain some of the other skills needed for the job. If mathematics is not currently one of their strengths, they should try to work on their skills. They can do this not only by taking the required math classes in school but also by paying attention in those classes, asking questions of the teacher, studying at home, and completing assignments. Getting some (hopefully free) help from friends or relatives could help, too.

Math skills need to be second nature for pipelayers. This may not be the case when they're just starting out and hand-digging with shovels. But, eventually, when they have to operate the equipment, read blueprints, or even verify their timesheet and pay, they'll need to have a good knowledge of and fluency with numbers. Keep in mind, too, that many problem-solving skills are also taught in math class. Think about those story problems that many students cringe at when they pop up in a math assignment. Practicing solving those types of problems helps a person develop a logical mindset that is necessary for quick and effective decision-making on a job site.

If a person doesn't feel that he or she has good communication skills, there are many ways to improve. English and language arts classes are one free way that all high school students have at their fingertips. Don't think you have to be a grammarian, either, because you certainly do not. Getting a

High schools, trade schools, and colleges offer opportunities to learn necessary construction and engineering skills from knowledgeable instructors. Any technical instruction can be helpful in keeping your skills sharp.

handle on the basic skills of reading, writing, and listening can be beneficial for any job. Pipelaying is no different.

Keep in mind that some schools offer business English classes for students interested in business or vocational careers. A student entering the workforce after graduation would take this type of class instead of a traditional language arts course—or a higher level Advanced Placement (AP) course—that is meant for students who are going on to a four-year university. Business English focuses on writing and reading tasks that people encounter in the workforce: writing emails, building résumés, and preparing for interviews. Students interested in this option should speak with their high school counselor to see if such a class is offered at their school.

Another great option to consider during (and after) high school is to take the time to develop the physical strength and agility needed on the job. Take some weight training classes or join a gym to develop overall strength. Add cardio to an exercise routine to increase endurance, since working on a

A high school career counselor or guidance counselor can provide valuable information, including providing tips for finding information online, for students who want to research jobs in hands-on fields such as pipelaying.

pipeline job site is a physically demanding job that can take its toll. To develop agility, try incorporating calisthenics and even disciplines like yoga into a daily routine, or at least several times a week.

WORK STUDY OR VOCATIONAL EDUCATION

In some high schools, work-study and vocational education is available to students. In work-study courses, students get to go to a job site for part of their school day and actually get high school credit for their work—oftentimes along with a paycheck. This allows students to get training in all kinds of fields before they are even out of high school. The great part about these programs is that when students in these programs graduate from high school, they are often eligible for even higher-paying positions because they have at least a year (or more) of experience and training under their belt. In the field of construction, work-study can be in any type of project: house building, landscaping, painting, cement work, plumbing, and so forth. If work-study isn't an option, teens can always look into getting a part-time, after-school job or summer job in the construction industry in order to get some experience before graduation.

Some high schools also have vocational education (vo-tech) programs. In these programs, students take classes at the school that teach various hands-on skills. Vocational education often includes elements like wood shop, automotive repair, drafting, and even house construction, among others. While schools may not specifically have pipelaying classes, taking any kind of hands-on course is bound to be helpful for a future pipelayer. In the vocational education classes, students learn how to apply the math skills they have developed in other classes. They learn how to use various types of machines, tools, and equipment. And they become familiar with the process of decision-making and problem-solving. The more experience a person has in all of this, the better, and will only aid in his or her future goals in a pipelaying career.

BEYOND HIGH SCHOOL

But what about after high school? What if you never took any of these classes and don't have any experience in construction, but still want to get a job in this line of work? The answer to this is fairly simple: just apply for basic entry-level jobs, at any age. Don't be shy about the fact that you don't have experience. If you have a willingness to work hard and have a good attitude about gaining some new skills, most contractors would be happy to give you a chance.

If you feel that you'd like to have a little help with some of the math and communication skills and don't feel you can learn those on the job, then you could always take a few classes at a community college or even brush up by enrolling in evening classes. There may even be free online classes that you can take, too. Google the phrase "free math classes" and see what results you get.

There are also trade tech schools that offer classes related to the construction industry. Conduct an online search with such phrases as "trade tech schools" or "schools for construction" and see what results for your area. YouTube videos are also a great resource. You can find ones on nearly any how-to topic you can imagine. So, if you want to learn how to use a laser level, for example, then just Google it. There's sure to be a video or two (or twenty) that will show you how. One important thing to remember is to always put safety first. Do not try to

Online resources, such as commercial job-search sites and government pages dedicated to workforce development, are among the most useful ones for finding out about trade schools and job opportunities.

imitate what people do in videos without adult supervision if it involves using power tools or other equipment. If you have any doubts or questions about whether something online is something to safely emulate, ask a trusted adult, whether it's a relative, teacher, mentor, or boss.

BEGINNER'S TRAINING ON HEAVY EQUIPMENT

Don't expect that your first day on the job as a laborer with no experience will land you in the seat of heavy equipment. The likelihood of that happening is very slim. These machines are not only extremely expensive, but they can also be very dangerous. It takes a great amount of training, time, and practice to become truly proficient in their use.

There are several ways for people to obtain training on heavy equipment. The first is by getting hired as a laborer and then asking to be trained on the machines during downtime on the job. This route is a very common one. It's also cost-effective, since the worker gets paid training. Another advantage here is that it is more or less like being an apprentice. You're getting trained by experts in the field who handle such machines on a daily basis.

Another way to get trained on the machines is to take classes. There are several schools around the country that specialize in heavy equipment training. Perform a Google search to see what

Dressing warmly is essential for many pipelaying projects, which may be outside in cold weather. Layers are essential because conditions on the job site can change throughout the day.

type of options might be available to you in your area. Do your homework, though, on these programs. Figure out how much they will cost. If you have to shell out thousands or tens of thousands of dollars to get trained, then it probably will not be worth it to go this route. It'll take you too long to earn that much money back on the job.

HEAVY EQUIPMENT OPERATOR TRAINING: JAMES HUDSON

James Hudson, a substitute teacher in San Diego, recently became curious about what it would take to become a heavy equipment operator. He had often driven by job sites and had been interested in learning how to operate the big equipment that he saw. He Googled the phrase, "how to become a heavy equipment operator." One of his results was for the local Caterpillar dealership that offered classes on how to operate such equipment.

This particular dealership taught students how to operate the bulldozer, backhoe, skid-steer, motor grader, and wheel loader. Hudson decided to take two of the courses, each of which cost him several hundred dollars to complete. When he had successfully completed the courses, he received a certificate that proved his ability to operate those particular types and sizes of machines.

Hudson explains on his YouTube channel that workers can also get hired as a laborer at a construction company. During downtime, they can have one of the equipment operators train them how to use the equipment. "That way, if someone is sick or someone quits, you can jump in and take that position. Then, they can hire a laborer to replace you for the position that you are leaving," he explains.

He was particularly excited about taking training courses because now he can work part-time as a heavy equipment operator to supplement his income from his regular job. "For all of the school breaks throughout the year, I like to do construction work during my breaks. The pay is great and there are usually plenty of opportunities for work," he said.

In addition to financial concerns, you'll also want to ask about the instructors in any program you apply to. Do they have real-world construction site experience, or have they only ever worked at the school? You want to be trained by a person who has actually worked (for many years, preferably) on a job site, not just in a school environment.

You'll also want to inquire about the amount of time you'll get to spend on the equipment versus simply indoor classroom time. How many machines are available for the number of students? Reading books about machines is really not enough, and any reputable and useful program will have plenty of hands-on training.

Pipelayers may learn a variety of skills on the job, including getting guidance on basic maintenance of the heavy machinery and vehicles they may encounter on job sites.

An advantage of taking courses is that you'll receive official certifications at the end that show your competency on the machines. With those in hand, you can go out and immediately start applying for the higher-paying heavy equipment operator jobs instead of having to settle for entry-level laborer positions.

CHAPTER FOUR

LANDING A JOB

Just ask any job seeker and he or she will tell you that one of the worst parts of finding a job is the beginning job search! That's because many people just simply don't know where to begin. This chapter is designed to give you a few tools to put in your job-searching belt.

ONLINE JOB SEARCHES

In today's work force, the most common way to look for a job is online. Job boards such as Monster.com, Indeed .com, Simplyhired.com, and ConstructionJobs.com are great places to get started. Hop on any of these sites, type in "laborer," "pipelayer," "heavy equipment operator," or any other term that suits your interest, and check out the results. These are all nationwide job boards, so the results can range all over the country. This may be an advantage to you if you're eager to relocate. However, if you want to find jobs only in your current area, all of these sites allow you to narrow your search to your zip code or surrounding ones.

Formal business attire, or clothing, isn't necessary for a construction-related job interview. Make sure to dress neatly, smile, and look your interviewers in the eyes, however.

Remember that online job searches are just the beginning. According to an article about job websites on Balance.com, "Career coaches recommend spending no more than 10 percent of your job searching time online." The bulk of a searcher's time should be out in the real world "generating leads, networking, researching companies, and meeting people face to face."

ANALYZING A JOB POSTING

One of the great things about job postings either online or on a physical job board is seeing what a pipelayer's responsibilities typically are. If you're just breaking into this job sector, you can use these lists as a base for your training goals. Let's say a company includes some of these tasks on their job posting for pipelayer:

- Check slopes for conformation to requirements, using levels or lasers
- Cover pipes or boxes with earth or other materials
- Connect pipe or box pieces and seal joints, using welding equipment, cement, or glue
- Cut pipes or boxes to required lengths
- Install and repair sanitary and storm water sewer structures and pipe systems
- Install and use instruments such as lasers, grade rods, and transit levels
- Grade and level trench bases, using tamping machines and hand tools

You can now go through this list one by one and ask yourself these questions: Do I know how to do this? If not, is there some way that I can learn the basics before the interview (e.g., asking a friend on the job to teach you, watching YouTube videos, taking a class, reading How-To tips online)? Or, if I can't learn these things ahead of time, can I convince the company that I'm eager and willing to learn?

The internet provides a world of job-seeking opportunities. Don't worry if you don't have a computer, smartphone, or internet access. You can access both at most public libraries and at most schools.

NETWORKING

Job seekers should also remember to leverage their most powerful resources: their own personal networks of friends and family. Some people feel too awkward about doing this. They feel that they're putting their friends and family on the spot to find them a job, so they just keep quiet and avoid asking them altogether.

Asking for such favors works if you approach it the right way. It's best to avoid telling someone, "Hey, I want a job, get me hired at your company." Such a request may make people feel uncomfortable if they don't want to do it, for whatever reason. Instead, approach it like this, "I'm really interested in getting a job in the construction industry. If you ever hear of anyone looking to hire, would you mind letting me know?" In that case, there's little pressure on the person you're talking to. You're also starting out the conversation by expressing a real interest that you have and concluding it with a request that's more low key.

If you don't feel comfortable doing this in person, you can always send out texts, emails, or messages on social media to your contacts. Just be sure to make it personal. Don't send out a mass email or mass text, unless you are following up after a few instances of making contact. A cold mass email could just annoy the recipients and will likely not lead to much successful networking.

OUT IN THE COLD

Have you ever heard of the term "cold calling"? This is a term generally used by salespeople when they call individuals or companies that they don't know to ask questions or sell a product. Cold calling isn't just for sales—it can also be an effective tool in job searching. Keep in mind that it doesn't have to involve just calling on the phone either. You can call on companies by emailing or visiting them in person, too.

One way to handle a call like this is to say something like this: "Hi, My name is ________. I live here locally and I'm really interested in working for your company. Could you tell me the process of applying for a position as a pipelayer, heavy equipment operator, laborer, etc.?" At that point, they may just direct you to their job board or tell you they're not hiring. But before you hang up the phone or leave the office, try to get some information from them by asking such questions as, "When is the best time to look for a job with your company?" "Do you hire seasonally?" "What positions are usually the most in demand?"

TEMPORARY OR STAFFING SERVICES

Instead of going directly to the company itself, you may want to consider visiting a local temporary (temp) or staffing service for work. These companies serve as the middle man between companies and employees. Many companies like to use them because they take care of the insurance, taxes, hiring, and firing of workers so that companies do not have to deal with these tasks.

When companies need temporary workers or seasonal workers, they will often go to a staffing company to fill those needs. If the company likes your performance on the job, they may just hire you directly on a full-time basis. To find these companies in your own area, conduct an online search using such phrases as "temp services," "staffing services," "temp agencies," or even "construction jobs at temp services."

Bring copies of your résumé to any interview, even if you emailed one to the prospective employers before. Make sure it is easy to read and free of errors.

BUILDING YOUR RÉSUMÉ

Finding a job to apply for is the first step. The real process begins when you actually apply for it. Many companies will have a pen and paper application for you to fill out—for example, if you show up in person at a job fair or an open house. An application will include your basic information (name, address, birthday, and so forth) as well as a questionnaire-type list that asks about your experience, certification, education, and training. Other companies might ask that you fill out such applications online, via their websites or ones approved by them.

In addition to completing the company's application, it is essential that you put together your own résumé. You probably already know that a résumé is a professional document that briefly lists your education, work experience, talents, personality traits, and skills. Print your résumé on good quality paper, use standard fonts and layouts (like Times New Roman or Arial), and try to limit it to one page. Two pages is the absolute maximum. At this point, some new job applicants may ask, "But what about me? I don't have anything to put on a résumé because I've never worked in this industry. I have no experience."

INTERVIEW THE INTERVIEWER

Interviews are seen as the time that an employer gets to know the applicant to see if he or she is a good fit for the job. However, interviews should really be seen as a two-way street. Not only should the employer be assessing the fit of the applicant for the position, but the applicant should also be determining whether or not this company is right for him or her.

Interviewing experts recommend that applicants come to the interview with a few questions of their own. They also recommend that applicants take some time to research the company before the interview, so the questions can be better tailored for the particular position and company. The following are questions that applicants might ask of the interviewer. Avoid asking too many, and thus taking too much time from the interviewer, or convincing them you know little about the job in question. The experts recommend asking only two or three. Here are a few examples to choose from:

1. What do you like best about working for this company?
2. What are your expectations for a person in this role over the first month? First six months? Year?
3. What do you feel are the most important qualities for someone to do well in this job?
4. Will there be opportunities for learning additional skills (heavy equipment operation and tool training, leadership opportunities, and so forth)?
5. How do you define success for this job?
6. Can I have a quick tour or meet some of the people I'd be working with?

(continued on the next page)

(continued from the previous page)

7. What is the average length of time that employees stay with this company?
8. Will I be mentored in this position?
9. Will I have opportunities in the future to mentor others?
10. How will you judge my success in the job?
11. What's the most important thing I can complete in the first thirty days of my time on the job?
12. What are the next steps in the interview process?
13. When should I expect to hear back about this position?

It may feel like you don't have anything to include on a résumé, but you actually do. Even someone right out of high school can prepare a good one. Here are some ideas of details you can include on each part:

- **Education**: List your high school graduation date or expected graduation date. Or, you can state that you took the GED if that is the route you went. You can also detail some of the classes that you took that pertain to the position:

mathematics, communication courses, vocational classes, physical fitness, and so forth. Include any post–high school information in this section, too, as well as any construction training you've taken, completed, and been certification in.

- **Work Experience**. List any, or at least most, of the jobs you've had, even if they don't specifically apply to the job you're seeking. Mention any responsibilities you had on the job, too, that show your ability to lead, take on responsibility, train others, and so forth. For example, if you worked a fast-food job, mention the roles you had to train others, be in charge of money, or manage one part of the restaurant. You can even include volunteer work you've been part of. Did you help build a house for a mission trip? Include that detail. Mention any tools you used while completing those tasks—even if they don't specifically apply to the job you're currently seeking.
- **Talents**. Relate any sports you do, musical abilities, or any other hobbies you enjoy. These show details about your personality and may help the person looking over the application picture you as being a good fit for the job.
- **Personality Traits**. Describe your positive traits, such as "works well with a team," "dependable," "hard-working," "willing and eager to learn," "cooperative," "responsible," and "a problem solver."
- **Skills**. This is the place you can explain the specific skills you have that relate to the job. Do you have experience using certain tools? List those here. Do you know how to operate heavy equipment? List the machines here.

Follow up with the interviewer in an email or a mailed note of thanks. Thank him or her for the interview opportunity. Use the letter as a chance to put your name back into the interviewer's mind.

Can you lift a certain amount of weight easily? List that information here. Do you have rock-climbing skills? List it. Note: The last one, or something similar, is a great detail to add, especially when applying for pipelaying and trench-related jobs.

- **References**. Include a line that says, "References available upon request." Then, contact a few individuals who can vouch for your character, work experience, skills, and education. This could be a teacher, coach, former boss, close family friend, member of the clergy, or other person of authority with whom you have a good relationship. Don't choose family members. They don't make the best references because they're more biased toward you and your abilities and employers might not take their recommendations seriously.

CHAPTER FIVE

MOVING ON UP

As has been mentioned, the most common way to enter the field of pipelaying is as a laborer. The best part about entering at that level is there is only one way to go in the company, and that is up! There are many opportunities for advancement in this field. Laborers can rise in the ranks to heavy equipment operator, foreman, supervisor, superintendent, and project manager. Pipelayers can also stretch their entrepreneurial muscles and start their own business, too.

EMPLOYEE OF THE YEAR

The best way to advance in any job is to be a hard worker and always look for opportunities to improve and learn. Don't just be satisfied with the same old routine every day. Ask for new responsibilities (when ready for them), and do that often. Look at a job as more than just a paycheck. See it instead as a quality way to spend your time, where you not only get paid for your efforts, but you also get to learn new skills and improve yourself simultaneously.

Along with this hardworking mindset, you also must have a good attitude. Don't show up grumpy to work. Leave your personal problems at home. Do the tasks asked of you with

There are plenty of opportunities in construction to move up the ladder. Keep building your skills. Ask questions, and inquire about additional training. Demonstrate your professionalism and confidence when meeting with managers.

a positive perspective. Get along with your coworkers. Show respect to your boss—to his or her face and behind his or her back. Arrive early for your job. All of these tips will help you become that employee that no company wants to be without.

STAYING UP TO DATE

There's an old quote that says, "The only thing that is constant is change." This is true in all areas of life, especially jobs that deal with technology and engineering, like pipelaying. There

Pipelaying is labor intensive and can be repetitive. Good teamwork and a positive attitude can go a long way in keeping morale on the job site good.

will constantly be new ideas, machinery, and methods in this industry. And the best way to move up in the industry is to stay on top of your game. Subscribe to some of the top digital magazines and journals in the industry, such as *Equipment World*, *Construction Today*, *Civil Engineering*, and *Construction Week Online.* By reading these periodicals often, you'll be able to find out the latest in what's going on around the nation (and world) in the construction industry.

Another way to stay up-to-date is to follow industry-related blogs and Twitter handles for additional updates. Joining a construction-related group on LinkedIn can also be helpful. Not only will you be able to find out about the latest methods from the people in the industry, but you'll also be able to network with other professionals in the field across the nation (and the world). This can help you find out about job opportunities that may help you advance in the field.

You may also want to consider taking additional night classes to advance in the field. If you want to be a business owner, take some business classes. If you want to be a better manager or supervisor, look into classes that will help you develop leadership and teaching skills. As a heavy equipment operator, you can also get certified to operate larger and more powerful machines. The more machines you know how to operate, the more job security you'll have and the higher your wages will be.

NETWORKING AND MENTORING

Once you land the job, your need to network does not end. Constantly look for ways to connect with others in the industry without being pushy or overbearing. Develop a good rapport with your superiors and coworkers. Make connections with others outside your company: LinkedIn and other social networks are potential resources for this. Seek out someone you respect in the industry—a mentor—and ask questions and advice. Make your name known in a positive way. Be that

Whether a supervisor on a job site, a teacher, or a counselor, a trusted and more experienced person at work or school can give you good advice on picking a job and how to land it.

person that everyone can mention and think, "Yeah, I know so-and-so. A great worker, good person. You should hire them!"

STAYING SAFE ON THE JOB

One way to make sure you have a chance to move up in a company is by staying safe on the job. If you get injured—or worse—then your days of being a pipelayer could be over.

ADVANCING IN CONSTRUCTION: ADVICE FROM AN EXPERT

Kyle Riegle is a heavy equipment operator. He started out as a laborer. He recommends going to an excavating or landscaping company and applying for work. A landscaping company might be a better option to get on machines faster, especially the backhoe, skid-steer, and tractor. "You'll start out as a basic laborer with a shovel in your hand," he explains in one of his YouTube videos. "If you go to work for a company, you'll get paid to learn."

Riegle advises to show up for an interview excited, and eager to learn and advance. "Go into the interview and be up front about it," he suggests. "Say: 'Listen, I've never operated equipment, but I want to run equipment. I want to be that guy on the machines. I want to be your foreman. I want to be your supervisor. How do I get there with your company? How fast can that happen?' Talk to them about it. That's what I did," he explains. "If an eighteen-year-old kid straight out of high school came in and told me that, I would be like 'Heck yeah, I'm going to hire you!' I'd be all about it!"

(continued on the next page)

(continued from the previous page)

He further explains in his online interview that the best experience you can get is to have a foreman, supervisor, or heavy equipment operator teach you the equipment hand-in-hand. "When you get opportunities like that, treat them like pure gold," he advises. There's a lot to learn about digging around houses, gas lines, sewer lines. And the best people to teach you are the ones who do it expertly every day.

In addition to on-the-job training, Riegle also highly suggests getting a Class A commercial driver's license (CDL), which opens up all kinds of other opportunities for jobs.

In the United States, the Department of Labor monitors and regulates the safety industry through the Occupational Safety and Health Administration (OSHA). Inspectors will often come to job sites and make sure everything is up to code. If not, the job could be shut down for the safety of the workers.

Every industry has its safety rules and regulations. Get to know those required for the pipelaying industry. One definite hazard on the job is during trenching work. Trenches must be properly dug and secured before anyone gets inside of them. If not, the walls could collapse and the workers inside the trench could be injured, crushed, or buried alive.

Wearing proper clothing and hard hats is another necessary regulation to follow. Keep in mind that these rules aren't just there to make things more complicated on the job. They're

Take your role on an infrastructure team seriously. Your part is just as important as anyone else's in the overall project. There is a great sense of satisfaction in pulling together and doing a good job, with concrete results.

meant to keep everyone safe and allow everyone a chance to go home uninjured at the end of the workday.

A SENSE OF PRIDE

Jobs in the construction industry can be physically demanding and mentally challenging. But that is exactly what attracts many people to them. Pipelayers may leave at the end of the day completely exhausted, but they also leave knowing that they've completed real tasks in the real world that help real people. And what can be more rewarding than that?

BUREAU OF LABOR STATISTICS TIPS

- Industry sectors that pipelayers work in: Utility system construction; local government; building equipment contracting; specialty trade contracting; highway, street, and bridge construction; utility system construction; water and sewage; land subdivision; residential and nonresidential building construction; natural gas distribution; electric power generation.
- Earning potential: For pipelayers, average wages and overtime pay can make it a comfortable living for most workers throughout the nation. More experienced pipelayers and supervisors earn a modest, middle-class salary.
- States with the highest wages for pipelayers: Massachusetts, Alaska, Illinois, New Jersey, Minnesota
- States with the most pipelayers: California, Texas, New York, Florida, Missouri, Tennessee, North Carolina, Virginia, Washington, Pennsylvania, Ohio, Alabama
- General duties: Lay pipe for storm or sanitation sewers, drains, and water mains. Perform any combination of the following tasks: grade trenches or culverts, position pipe, or seal joints.
- Nationally, as of about 2016, there are about 41,000 active pipelayer positions.

GLOSSARY

apprentice A worker who learns a trade by working alongside an experienced worker.

aquifer Underground rock formations that contain groundwater.

blueprint A design, plan, or technical drawing that details a structure, project, or machine.

crane A machine used to lift and move heavy objects.

foreman The leader of a construction crew or other group of physical laborers.

GED An acronym for General Educational Development. This is a test that an individual can take to show high school level proficiency instead of completing the coursework necessary for a diploma.

grader A machine that is used to level the ground.

laser A device that generates an intense beam of light.

level A measuring device used to reveal whether a surface is perfectly level or plumb.

networking Connecting with people as a way to exchange ideas, be introduced to others, and learn new skills.

project manager The person in charge of managing the stages of a construction project from beginning to end.

qanats Underground tunnels used to transport water by the Mesopotamians.

résumé A listing of someone's education and experience provided to employers in order to procure work.

superintendent A manager on construction projects who runs day-to-day operations and manages the short-term scheduling.

supervisor A leader on a job site, usually superior to a foreman, who manages subcontractors, enforces codes, and meets construction budgets.

trench A long, narrow ditch where pipes are installed.

vo-tech Vocational education classes that prepare students for a specific job or career in the trades.

work study Opportunities in high school where students can get school credit while working at a job during the school day.

American Institute of Constructors
700 North Fairfax Street, Suite 510
Alexandria, VA 22314
(703) 683-4999
Website: http://professionalconstructor.site-ym.com
Twitter: @ProConstructors
Facebook: @aicccc
This professional society is a trade organization that provides opportunities for education and certification and establishes quality standards for the construction industry.

Canadian Apprenticeship Forum (CAF-FCA)
404-2197 Riverside Drive
Ottawa, ON K1H 7X3
Canada
(613) 235-4004
Website: http://caf-fca.org
Facebook: @cafapprenticeship
Twitter: @CAF_FCA
This nonprofit connects Canada's apprenticeship community: employers, unions, equity-seeking groups, educational institutions, and jurisdictions support CAF-FCA.

International Union of Operating Engineers (IUOE)
1125 17th Street NW
Washington, DC 20036
(202) 429-9100

Website: http://www.iuoe.org
In operation since 1896, this trade union represents the interests of its members with more than 120 local unions throughout the United States and Canada. It also offers courses at more than one hundred training centers throughout both countries.

IUOE Canada
350 Sparks Street, Suite 1102
Ottawa, ON K1R 7S8
Canada
(613) 567-5544
Website: http://www.iuoe.org/about-iuoe/iuoe-canada
This website takes you to the Canadian branch of IUOE and will be of particular interest to workers employed on construction projects in Canada.

National Association of Women in Construction (NAWIC)
327 S. Adams Street
Fort Worth, TX 76104
(817) 877-5551
Website: http://www.nawic.org
NAWIC was founded in 1953 by women working in construction. This organization provides educational opportunities, networking services, and professional development. There are approximately two hundred chapters across the United States.

NCCER (formerly National Center for Construction Education and Research)
13614 Progress Boulevard
Alachua, FL 32615
(888) 622-3720
Website: http://www.nccer.org
Facebook/Twitter/Instagram: @NCCER
YouTube: @nccerus
Established in 1996, NCCER is a nonprofit education foundation that is dedicated to improving the training of workers in the construction industry, with a standardized training program for curricula in seventy craft areas.

Occupational Safety and Health Administration (OSHA)
US Department of Labor
200 Constitution Avenue NW
Washington, DC 20210
(800) 321-OSHA (6742)
Website: http://www.osha.gov
Facebook: @departmentoflabor
Twitter and Instagram: @USDOL
OSHA is a division of the US Department of Labor, which helps keep workers safe on the job by requiring companies to maintain safety standards for their workers.

FOR FURTHER READING

Byers, Ann. *A Career as a Construction Manager* (Essential Careers). New York, NY: Rosen Publishing, 2016.

Capachi, Nick, and John Capachi. *Excavation and Grading Handbook*. Carlsbad, CA: Craftsman Book Company, 2005.

Carter, W. Hodding. *Flushed: How the Plumber Saved Civilization*. New York, NY: Atria Books, 2007.

Jackson, Barbara J. *Construction Management Jump Start: The Best First Step Toward a Career in Construction Management*. Hoboken, NJ: Sybex, 2010.

Johnson, Anne. *Helper Pipelayer, Plumber, Pipefitter & Steamfitter Career* (Special Edition). Careers Collection, CreateSpace Independent Publishing Platform, 2016.

Joyce, Michael A. *Blueprint Reading and Drafting for Plumbers*. Farmington Hills, MI: Cengage Learning, 2008.

Leavitt, Amie Jane. *The Vo-Tech Track to Success in Architecture and Construction* (Learning a Trade, Preparing for a Career). New York, NY: Rosen Publishing, 2015.

McKeon, John K. *Becoming a Construction Manager*. Hoboken, NJ: John Wiley, 2011.

NCCER. *Heavy Equipment Operations, Level 1 Trainee Guide*. Upper Saddle River, NJ: Prentice Hall, 2012.

Nichols, Herbert, and David Day. *Moving the Earth: The Workbook of Excavation*. 6th ed. New York, NY: McGraw-Hill Professional, 2010.

Raczon, Frank, and Keith Haddock. *Caterpillar: Modern Earthmoving Marvels*. Minneapolis, MN: Motorbooks, 2015.

Roberts, Dave. *Pipe & Excavating Contracting Revised*. Carlsbad, CA: Craftsman Book Company, 2011.

Smith, Lee. *Mathematics for Plumbers and Pipefitters*. Farmington Hills, MI: Cengage, 2012.

BIBLIOGRAPHY

Allseas.com. "Off Shore Careers." Retrieved September 29, 2017. https://allseas.com/careers/offshore.

Cady, Staley. *The Separate System of Sewerage*. New York, NY: D. Van Nostrand, Co., 1899.

CareerIgniter.com. "How to Become a Construction Foreman." Retrieved October 5, 2017. http://www.careerigniter.com/careers/construction-foreman.

Civilcareers. "Pipe Laying." August 25, 2008. https://www.youtube.com/watch?v=eyWVozHMKLY.

Copper Development Association, Inc. "Discovering Copper Online." Retrieved September 15, 2017. https://www.copper.org/publications/newsletters/discover/2005/march/article2.html March 2005.

Doyle, Allison. "Top 10 Best Job Websites: Maximizing Your Online Job Search." TheBalance.com. July 5, 2017. https://www.thebalance.com/top-best-job-websites-2064080

Hudson, James. "How to Become a Heavy Equipment Operator." May 29, 2017. https://www.youtube.com/watch?v=sLVv9AtHzzg.

Natural Gas Supply Association. "Natural Gas History." Retrieved September 15, 2017. http://naturalgas.org/overview/history/.

Offshore Fleet: Offshore Industry and Technology Journal. "Pipelaying Vessel." Retrieved September 29, 2017. http://offshore-fleet.com/data/pipelay-vessel.htm.

Riegle, Kyle. "How to Become a Heavy Equipment Operator." April 17, 2016. https://www.youtube.com/watch?v=ELXylfDEHQY.

Study.com. "How to Become a Construction Superintendent." Retrieved October 8, 2017. http://study.com/articles/How_to_Become_a_Construction_Superintendent_Career_Roadmap.html.

UNESCO. "The Persian Qanat." Retrieved September 15, 2017. http://whc.unesco.org/en/list/1506.

United States Department of Labor: Occupational Safety and Health Administration (OSHA) "Worker Safety Series." Retrieved October 13, 2017. https://www.osha.gov/Publications/OSHA3252/3252.html.

"Watering Ancient Rome." *Nova*, February 22, 2000. http://www.pbs.org/wgbh/nova/ancient/roman-aqueducts.html.

INDEX

M

N

O

P

Q

R

S

ABOUT THE AUTHOR

Amie Jane Leavitt graduated from Brigham Young University and is an accomplished author, researcher, and photographer. She has written numerous books for young readers, has contributed to online and print media, and has worked as a consultant, writer, and editor for educational publishing and assessment companies.

PHOTO CREDITS

Cover, p. 3 pryzmat/Shutterstock.com; pp. 6–7 © iStockphoto.com/timhughes; p. 11 De Agostini Picture Library/Bridgeman Images; p. 13 withGod/Shutterstock.com; p. 16 nostal6ie/Shutterstock.com; p. 18 Gena Melendrez/Shutterstock.com; p. 20 Nielskliim/Shutterstock.com; p. 23 ESB Professional/Shutterstock.com; p. 24 Kirill Kudryavtsev/AFP/Getty Images; p. 28 adyinmutlu/E+/Getty Images; p. 31 © iStockphoto.com/Antonio_Diaz; p. 33 Kaesler Media /Shutterstock.com; p. 37 Huntstock/Getty Images; pp. 38, 48 asiseeit/E+/Getty Images; pp. 40, 64 Hero Images/Getty Images; p. 43 AlexKZ/Shutterstock.com; p. 46 Monty Rakusen/Cultura/Getty Images; p. 50 WayHome studio/Shutterstock.com; p. 53 George Rudy/Shutterstock.com; p. 58 © iStockphoto.com/Rawpixel; p. 61 sirtravelalot/Shutterstock.com; p. 62 Andrea Slatter/Shutterstock.com; p. 67 deela dee/Shutterstock.com; interior pages background (pipes) N.Surisuk/Shutterstock.com.

Design: Nelson Sá; Layout: Nicole Russo-Duca; Editor: Phil Wolny; Photo Researcher: Karen Huang